The Characters of the Crucifixion

Joseph Fichtner, O.S.C.

Illustrated by
Mary Charles McGough, O.S.B.

A Liturgical Press Book

THE LITURGICAL PRESS
Collegeville, Minnesota
www.litpress.org

Cover design by Ann Blattner. Illustrations by Mary Charles McGough, O.S.B.

1   2   3   4   5   6   7   8

Library of Congress Cataloging-in-Publication Data

Fichtner, Joseph.
    The characters of the Crucifixion / Joseph Fichtner.
        p. cm.
    ISBN 0-8146-2360-3 (alk. paper)
        1. Jesus Christ—Passion. I. Title.
    BT431 .F53 2000
    232.96—dc21   00-021672

Contents

Preface   v

Scriptural References to the Passion Narrative
   and Related Passages   viii

1 Peter   1

2 Judas Iscariot   6

3 The High Priests   10

4 Pontius Pilate   14

5 The Crowd of Spectators   18

6 Barabbas   22

7 Roman Soldiers   25

8 Simon of Cyrene   29

9 Women of Jerusalem   32

10 The Mother of the Zebedees   36

11 The Two Thieves   40

12 Mary Magdalene   44

13 John, Son of Zebedee   47

14 Mary, Mother of Jesus   51

15 Christ Crucified   55

Epilogue   59

Preface

I chanced upon the article "Divining the American Character," its present and future, when a friend brought me a number of issues of *The Wall Street Journal*, which devoted several pages to it in one of its quarterly surveys titled "American Opinion" (March 5, 1998). Curiously, the survey uses the term "divining," which means to discover or declare by divination; prophesy. "Divining" suggests that one looks at the national character from a divine point of view. The survey, however, doesn't view Americans, private and public, mainly according to religious or moral criteria, but rather political, economic, cultural, and social. In fact, the substance of the survey is polled from two thousand adults, interviewed by telephone nationwide and in proportion to population.

The religious, moral issue of the "character" rated the lowest percentage, and as a whole it was seen to be on the decline, regrettably. Yet we should not discount in every human being the "transcendent" character which makes man "mysteriously different" from every other creature, as Pope John Paul II writes in his encyclical The Gospel of Life.

Here are character studies which depend on gospel information, the characterizations drawn from scriptural details. Even though they may seem sketchy, there is little, if anything, of legend (nothing at all of poll-value!) here. The gospel writers are interested in the historical backgrounds and life-situations of the persons, as told principally in the passion narrative, the earliest and longest piece of the Gospel. The characterizations in the Scriptures themselves are very much up front—no cover-ups as do occur in the current distinction between private life and public role. To be truth-seeking we must ask ourselves about the responsibility for crucifying Christ and discern the human and the divine character of the event.

In the two thousand years of evangelization and the re-evangelization promoted by Pope John Paul II, the Church still has to face the mystery of the human personality because every person is created in the image and likeness of God and reflects his mystery. It is in, through, and with Christ, after whom we are patterned, that we are to "divine" ourselves. He is the *crux* of every human character, and his cross characteristic of *violent* death.

And yet, humanly speaking, we tend to see ourselves, by comparison and distinction, in the mirror of other persons with their distinctive characteristics. Traits such as respect, compassion, responsibility, kindness, self-discipline, and integrity are worth looking into, climaxing in the love of God and neighbor.

I invite the reader to a self-examination in the context of the crucifixion, very real, heart-rendering and mind-boggling. Hopefully it can be a character-building experience. By reading and reflecting upon the passion narrative we are led to consider ourselves "character witnesses."

In the four Gospels we encounter people both good and bad. The Gospel of Christ presents this catalogue of them, and they represent various walks of life. That explains why we include the bad or unsavory who are gathered around the cross of Christ. Flawed characters are the cause of it, and they symbolize the evil spirit that still dwells among us and threatens us. They manifest the black and white sides of the human make-up. But by force of grace and example Christ draws good out of evil. What the apostle Peter says to married women of his day is true for all of us, that "adornment is rather the hidden character of the heart, expressed in the unfading beauty of a calm and gentle disposition" (1 Pet 3:4).

It is advisable to read the scriptural references to the persons here before our characterizations of them. We must put aside any and all preconceived notions about them, because the sorting of people is somewhat debatable. This is a look at human life at the start of the first millennium, and its reflection in our own.

The great Anglican preacher John Henry Newman, in the heyday of his preaching, focused at times on persons of the Old and New Testaments and had them published in his *Parochial and Plain Sermons.* They are still well worth reading, conveying biblical grace and truth in an incomparable English style. We may take a cue from him by reading and studying not only lives of the saints but characters who emerge from the biblical pages.

We should like to know more details about the last hours of Jesus' life, about the men and women who accompanied him on the way of the cross. Not merely out of curiosity but to be closer to them in the mystery of our salvation.

The crucifixion-event has a unique "character" of itself, the mystery of the cross, in which we all are involved as collaborators, unrestricted in time.

The "biblical" persons are described here, not "divined," leaving something to the imagination. Though they are very much up to date in the Gospel, the consequences of their life and action do continue to break out of eternity into time.

Joseph Fichtner, O.S.C.
Crosier Community of Phoenix

Scriptural References to the Passion Narrative and Related Passages

Matt 16:21-28; 17:22-23; 20:17-19; 26:1-75; 27:1-65; 28:1-15

Mark 8:34-38; 9:30-32; 10:32-34; 14:1-72; 15:1-47; 16:1-20

Luke 9:22, 43-45; 22:34, 39-71; 23:1-56; 24:1-12

John 2:1-5; 12:1-8, 23-28; 13:21-30; 17:1-26; 18:1-40; 19:1-42; 20:1-18

1

Peter

When we first meet Peter in the Gospel we may be somewhat puzzled by him. To get to know him better we have to follow him as he keeps himself at a distance from Christ on his way of the cross.

He may mystify us because in the course of time he fills many shoes, and his tracks on land and water are hidden in time. There is more to his careers than we can learn from the sources. Images of Peter are numbered—to quote one source: "missionary fisherman, pastoral shepherd, martyr, recipient of special revelation, confessor of the true faith, magisterial protector, and repentant sinner." The portraits are certainly not in historical order, are they?

As we page through the Gospel accounts of him, the Acts of the Apostles, and his letter(s), he seems to gain prominence and be more representative of the disciples of Jesus than speaking and acting as an individual (unless he declares to them, "I'm going fishing").

He's one of the first to be called by Christ out of his native element, the Sea of Galilee, to be a "fisher of men." Wherever he travels afterward his accent betrays him as a Galilean. But it should not deter us from understanding something of his speech and character.

He is first introduced to us by the name of Simon. The son of Jonah, is it surprising to him how many other "titles" are bestowed upon him in the course of time? Especially since names or titles are so meaningful, even sacred in Jewish tradition? They are not imposed on anyone by happenstance; they are to "characterize" someone, similar to the way we nickname someone familiar to us.

Simon is surnamed Peter by Christ to indicate what role he is to have in the Church. The name "Peter," which means "rock," suggests naturally how true, solid, and faithful a character Simon Peter must prove himself to be, the rock-foundation of the Church. If we trace this renaming further into Israelite history, we see that it is based upon God himself: "Who is a rock but our God?" Israel knew God to be a source of strength and safety.

The switch in his roles isn't easy for Peter to make, furthermore, if he is to *follow* his master. When Jesus predicts his own trial and sentence to death, Peter won't hear of it. Speaking up then and there, Peter is called "satan" (= "stumbling block") by Christ. When it comes to a real showdown, however, even though others in the company are shaken in their faith, Peter vouches to die with Christ.

The change-over from fisherman to "shepherd," for instance, demands that he be pastor for a whole flock of people, much more in public view and hearing than he had ever been. For the shepherd to *feed* his sheep in ecclesiastical pastureland symbolizes preaching and teaching. He is to be an inspirational, instructional, and protective leader. Above all he protects his sheep from straying into heresy, i.e., guarding their faith in Christ and in his Church.

Peter is at his worst and at his best in his leadership role. Christ foretells that Peter at his best will succeed his master to the point of martyrdom, and his death will glorify God. It will go to show how magnanimous a character he is. When on

Mount Tabor, earlier, in an exhilarating scene, he wants to set up three memorials: for Christ, Moses, and Elijah. And again in the triple protestation of love for his master, shortly before his triple denial of knowing the "man"—when he's at his worst.

As one belonging to Christ's inner circle of three apostles, Peter is with Christ during his agony in the Garden of Gethsemane. Whatever the reason, the three of them fall asleep while Jesus is off by himself to pray that the will of his Father be done in his behalf. He finds the three unwilling to watch and pray.

Later, after Jesus has been betrayed to the religious authorities for thirty pieces of silver, Peter comes to the defense of Jesus in a Kidron Valley garden. He draws his sword from his sheath and impulsively strikes off the high priest's servant's right ear (tradition names the servant "Malchus"). We are left to wonder how this fisherman-shepherd comes in possession of that bit of armor.

Peter, now weaker and more cowardly than before, trails Jesus at a distance as he is led to trial by the religious authorities. In his triple denial of knowing Jesus personally, he shows himself to be a stone of stumbling for Jesus—a scandal. We see something of the dark side of his character, how fallible he can be. His denials grow more emphatic and end up in a curse upon himself. By his own following of Jesus from afar and his denials, Peter raises some questions for ourselves, as we shall see.

Fortunately for Peter, he remembers Jesus' prediction of his denials and departs in tears. "I am a sinful man," he once confessed to Jesus. He retains his faith in Jesus, committed to him, unlike Judas who commits suicide in an act of despair. In contrast to Judas, Peter will die for Christ and in witness to his Church.

This rugged character of a fisherman-shepherd has his appeal and attraction, his excellences. He's rambunctious at times, no doubt, blurts out in moments of excitement, not knowing exactly what to say. Afloat with a big haul of fish and told that Jesus is waiting for him, he doesn't hesitate to jump from boat into water and swim ashore. His quick act recalls the other occasion in his life when he "walks" upon water and then, losing trust, begins to sink.

Perhaps because of his fishing experience, Peter is an observant and alert fellow. He's the one who notices the fig tree withered because it fails to bear fruit. He catches on quickly as Jesus questions his love (a triple protestation of love to reverse his triple denial). And at the Last Supper he wants to know from John the Beloved who Christ's betrayer is.

We should not bypass his home at Capernaum, how open and hospitable and family-spirited it is, indicative of how the early "house-churches" were to be, and the fact that his mother-in-law is living with him and being taken care of there. Capernaum, besides, is the center of his, Jesus', preaching-and-teaching excursions.

At the last he even takes the evangelist Mark under his wing and helps him in the composition of his Gospel. Peter gives him insight into the human side of Christ.

We can take as a closing scene upon his life the surprising haul of fish from the Sea of Tiberias, the morning after a night of failure. At Jesus' order, Peter doesn't only bring *some* fish but the *whole* catch, by actual count 153. The scene is so symbolic: boat (the Church), net (its mission), the 153 fish (its universal or catholic sign and mission).

Reflection-prayer

Peter, to you who bore several titles in your lifetime, I'm tempted to add the American nickname "Rocky" to fit your tough-mindedness but soft-hearted character. As a veteran fisherman you could have declined to weather the storm of opposition to the early Church. You are still "captain of the ship" in the person of our pope.

I admire and appeal to you as a first chosen of disciples of Christ, a leading apostle, and a priest-victim follower of Jesus.

You, an apostolical character, have left us a sense of repentance after failing to progress spiritually, a sense nonetheless of belongingness to an apostolic church. We can never be sure of our apostolic thrust in the Church, any more than we can be sure of ourselves.

We too must stand up for the rights of the Church in the world, in the face of social and political misunderstanding of her nature and of persecution.

We pray for courageous and wise leadership in our Church, that we may be gathered in a spirit of unity and holiness.

Peter, you were among the first to bring the Gospel to the Gentiles; help us in our desire for new evangelization.

2

Judas Iscariot

Of itself the name "Judas" isn't infamous, for other Judases in Palestinian history were upright men. But the reputation attached to the name keeps it from being given to any boy. "Iscariot" may mean "treasurer," one in charge of making payments, and it fits the character we are about to size up.

Lover of money, Judas Iscariot, in his handling of it as a disciple of Jesus, is seen in the gospel story in an "out-of-character" contrast to Mary of Bethany who spent money on costly perfume for an anointing of Jesus. It is hard to imagine that Judas truly had a love of the poor, for whom he thought the money should have been spent. He may even be contrasted to the rich young man who once asked Christ what he "might do further" after keeping the commandments, and who turned away from Christ upon hearing he should give away his possessions.

Although Judas as the treasurer in the company of Jesus is dutifully bound to give alms to beggars at night, he lifts the money stealthily from the money-box and spends it in betrayal of his master. The thirty shekels he is paid for betraying Jesus, whatever its worth in dollars and cents nowadays (if counted by the current rate of exchange it amounts to $10.00), was the going price for a slave killed by accident.

Judas is both a thief and a grumbler, dissatisfied with his lot in life. He may have nationalistic ambitions associated with the name "messiah." Jesus declines the title because of its nationalistic and political connotations. Judas also has wrong-headed notions about the future kingdom which Jesus promises.

Jesus in kindness to his friend pronounces a blessing upon him as upon all the twelve apostles, that they shall sit upon twelve thrones in judgment upon the twelve tribes of Israel (one duty of a king in Israel is to judge). But he defends Mary of Bethany against Judas. He urges him to reflect on what he is about to do and calls him to repentance.

Does Judas feel humble when Jesus washes his feet before the Last Supper? He doesn't hesitate to receive Holy Communion, and then take his leave before Jesus expresses his heartfelt farewell to the other apostles.

Judas conspires with the Jewish leaders and negotiates with them behind the scenes. Together they seem to be blind to Jesus' popularity, unaware of the reputation he has as a miracle-worker, friend of the poor, healer of the sick, and savior of the dying.

From his companionship with Jesus, Judas knows of the Garden of Gethsemane at the Garden of Olives, that he used to pray there. Judas turns the normal kiss of respect, like that of a pupil for his rabbi, into a traitorous act. But for the band of Roman soldiers gathered there to take Jesus away, it was a useless sign of recognition. Jesus, with full knowledge and free will, is ready to leave the garden on his own.

Jesus greets Judas warmly as a friend and lets him know that in reality his betrayal and the arrest are happening because he lets it happen. Contrariwise, Judas' act of betrayal is instigated by Satan.

We must not forget that Jesus, if he will, can use his divine foreknowledge and keep control of the whole succession of events, and in every way fulfill the prophecies of Scripture. He foresaw his betrayal even a year before his trial.

Jesus, nonetheless, has a keen regard for Judas as an individual; Jesus is willing himself to die in order to save him. He regards Judas as a friend, he doesn't confront him as a judge. He doesn't exclude him from the salvation of humankind. To be excluded from the divine plan of salvation, it would have been better that Judas had not been born.

Details vary regarding the fate of Judas, excepting Haceldama, the name of the place—the field—of his burial. His suicidal death and place of burial fulfilled a scriptural prophesy. (Did the field belong to him?)

Or was he buried in the potter's field, the junk or refuse quarter of Jerusalem? The odorous trash there was kept burning, suggestive of hell fire.

In biblical history he remains "the merchant" of Jerusalem ready to sell his master for "a pound of flesh," his way of "playing politics." Though gifted by his master, chosen by him to be a select member of the apostleship, Judas by his suicide is no witness for us to Jesus' resurrection.

How are we to interpret the life of Judas, or ought we to leave it, as we must for all others, to divine judgment?

Judas does prompt humans to awe of his selection by and companionship with Christ as they follow the course of his life. Jesus doesn't need Judas' obedience, for later he is to be replaced by Matthias. Nobody ought to presume himself or herself so secure in the Christian faith as never to fail, or as if the Lord has no replacement. In any case, each human life offers no gain or loss to God.

Reflection-prayer

Insofar as I have committed sin, I too have betrayed Jesus and must confess my sinfulness.

I was "chosen" by Jesus in the sacrament of baptism to be a child of God and a brother or sister of his, and to belong to a priestly people.

(I became a priest-disciple of his in the sacrament of holy orders. I pray never to sell Jesus short.)

The attraction to money can lure us into a greed, perhaps stronger today than ever before in human history (because of a liberal capitalism?).

In itself money is meant to be a medium of exchange, though it is in its ramifications degrading us into a culture of death, into a suicidal society, into a cheapening of human life. Am I guilty of consumerism?

I pray, Lord, for a "loose-change" attitude toward "sordid gain" or "shameful profit" and, instead, to give of myself generously.

3

The High Priests

The role the High Priests assume in the trial and condemnation of Jesus is in some respects prophetic, for as enemies of his they foresee and foretell his death. The Jewish people, in fact, ascribed prophetic powers to the High Priest: Jesus must die.

The priestly office in Judaism—the Sanhedrin—is hereditary, constituting a caste, its members appointed from sacerdotal families to be chief priests. The High Priests in the past felt themselves to be, in the absence of kings, promoters of a theocracy and leaders by Judaic political authority. The policy then was a far cry from our American separation of Church and state. The Jerusalem Temple was not only a place of worship; it was also like a safety deposit box and had its own police force or security guard.

The priestly aristocracy of the past was sometimes reputed for intrigue, bribery, and love of money. Yet the High Priests were "first-class" citizens and had to be treated as such.

The High Priest is to marry only a virgin, an undefiled Israelite. He is to have no physical contact with death, which would make him ritually unclean. He is to be physically fit for priestly function, that is, of good appearance. The High Priest is consecrated by filling his hands with the sacred flesh of the sacrificial victim. He takes turns at the temple service, twenty-four courses in all, within which courses are to be found for other ranks, like the Levites. He himself belongs to the levitical priesthood of ancient Israelitic origin.

During the Roman regime High Priests are appointed to office by Roman authorities and, by political maneuver, keep the appointments within the family. So enviable is their power that it creates divisions among themselves and the Pharisees and the mass of people.

Within the lifetime of Jesus, the first High Priest we meet is Annas, whose influence is very great. He is looked up to, and the high priesthood is handed down to five of his sons and his son-in-law.

The High Priest's office is for life. Though his office was for life, Annas was deposed by the Romans in A.D. 15. Still, in a brief unofficial night inquiry he pre-judges Jesus. Annas asks Jesus about his accomplices and projects in order to get the "goods" on him, to see if he is accused of an anti-Roman plot.

His son-in-law, Joseph Caiaphas (A.D. 18–36), then takes over. The next morning Jesus is brought to trial before Caiaphas and the Sanhedrin. The Sanhedrin is a council of seventy-one members drawn from the chief priests, elders (laypeople), and scribes (who are expert legal advisers), and is presided over by the ruling High Priest.

Caiaphas regards Jesus jealously and questions him whether he is the Messiah, the Son of the Most High. Jesus has to be careful in answering this tricky question, for a double charge can be brought against him. If he claims to be the Messiah, implying the widespread notion of having national, political, and military power, he gets himself in trouble with the Romans. On the other hand, the title "Son of the Most High" incriminates him with the High Priest and other Jewish religious authorities. He is trapped in a "Catch-22."

Jesus is arraigned before the High Priest, the Sanhedrin, and the Jewish crowd, and is charged—out of ignorance—with blasphemy, the punishment for which the Jewish law requires death. (The title "Son of God" need not imply divinity, inasmuch as under the Old Law any believer in the one, true God is a "son" of his.)

One of the High Priest's officers illegally strikes Jesus with a stick because Jesus asks for witnesses in his behalf.

We bystanders see that the real culprits in trial before God are Caiaphas, his high-priestly clique, the Sanhedrin, with the violent, hostile Pharisees and the cynical, opportunist Sadducees. They foresee Jesus' death as in line with that of other prophets of old, Jeremiah for instance.

The trial as a whole exemplifies how humans, since incurring the guilt of original sin, and after accepting false testimonies, usurp divine power in condemning to death fellow human beings. In doing so, they refuse testimonies of God's love for his people.

Though the High Priests are responsible for the death sentence imposed on Jesus, they use pagans for their purpose; the Roman soldiers take charge of the execution.

Jesus is the High Priest in a perfect priesthood that is to last forever in the new Jerusalem, in heaven the Temple of God, the holy of holies. Jesus is to be seen in his priestly role over against the Hebrew High Priests, referring to them and their kind as "thieves and robbers," and replacing them and their animal sacrifices, and succeeding Melchisedek in that he is a priest forever.

Though representatives of God to the people, the High Priests implicitly prefer Caesar to their God and King.

Reflection-prayer

To address the High Priests in Israelite religion as "fellow" priests is a misnomer. We do have some kinship

with them as readers of the Old Testament and as representatives of religion, and we do intend to support ecu-
menical and interfaith dialogue. We are open to learning
from fellow believers.

We are thankful that in the early Church "even a
large group of priests were becoming obedient to the
faith" (Acts 6:7).

We want to stay clear, as Jesus did, of the entangle-
ment of religion with politics. Yet we do stand and pray
for freedom of religion, for abiding by ethical and moral
principles.

As members of the People of God, as a priestly
people, we should hope and pray to be wise guides to and
humble examples of our citizenry in a heavenly kingdom.

As American citizens we subscribe to the Declara-
tion of Independence by which "We hold these Truths to
be self-evident, that all Men are created equal, that they
are endowed by their Creator with certain unalienable
Rights". . . and to the first article of the Constitution of
the United States, that "Congress shall make no law re-
specting an establishment of religion, or prohibiting the
free exercise thereof. . . ."

Do we intend to bear witness to Jesus and suffer
with him the affronts to faith and religion?

4

Pontius Pilate

P ontius Pilate has the distinction of being the most renowned *governor* in human history. Mind you, he was even known to us children as "Punches the Pilot"!

The adviser to the Roman emperor Tiberius appointed him a Judean (= Palestinian) prefect with headquarters at Caesarea on the Mediterranean coast. He ruled from A.D. 27 to 37, not only over Judea but Idumea and Samaria. His only other distinction is that his name was carved in a stone found at Caesarea in 1960.

Certainly the most noted—or should I say infamous?— event in his term of office is the trial of Jesus. It is held at the governor's tribunal, called *pretorium,* situated at the royal palace, Herod's residence, where he resided when in Jerusalem, where he could ask the advice of his council. It's questionable whether he actually did seek their advice. He was a stubborn, cruel, anti-Jewish ruler, with the supreme judicial power of sentencing to capital punishment, i.e., crucifixion.

The trial turns out to be a farce.

Pilate in his Roman province doesn't have to conduct the trial according to Roman criminal law. He can make his own rules or resort to custom. As a Roman official with financial and military jurisdiction, Pilate hesitates to interfere in matters of the Hebrew religion. The Jews, however, try to bring forward their religious charge under the cover of political offense, namely their charge against Jesus of claiming to be "a son of a god." They accuse Jesus too of claiming to be king of the Jews. The title, with its political connotations of rebellion against Rome prior to the Jewish war, Jesus refuses to take upon himself. Pilate acts out of fear of giving in to such a rebel movement. Thus in the end he simply hands Jesus over to his enemies, without formal charge, but having been told that his, Jesus' kingdom, is not of this world.

Pilate has little or no knowledge of Hebrew religious prejudices. He wants above all to be loyal to Rome, and that's why he fears a Jewish critical report to Rome, to the ultra-suspicious Tiberius. Upon conviction of Jesus, the terms of execution are reserved to Rome, so therefore the charge against him has to be political: the title assigned to Jesus, "king of the Jews."

The Jewish leaders rally the crowd of witnesses against Jesus even though they, or a great number of them, have seen or heard of Jesus performing miracles. Because he has insufficient evidence to convict him, Pilate is reluctant to condemn Jesus. He feels himself on unsteady footing, wobbling between the chief priests, the crowd, and his own convictions of Jesus' innocence, and three times he tries to set him free.

Pilate's Gentile wife has a dream about Jesus, innocent of any crime, and warns her husband to clear himself of the case. In front of the crowd crying for the death of Jesus, Pilate cavalierly washes his hands of the whole affair, as if washing his blood-guilt away. Is he nonetheless a "partner" in the crime because he doesn't heed his wife's "heaven-sent" warning?

It is also to be noted historically that Pilate had massacred Galileans, which put him in Herod's disfavor. But hearing that Jesus is a Galilean, it gives Pilate pause; he can refer the case to Herod Antipas. Before Herod Jesus remains silent, while the chief priests and scribes continue to keep Jesus on trial. The false charges against him do not prevent his enemies from mocking him as a king. Both Herod and Pilate hold Jesus to be innocent. The two Romans are ready to acquit Jesus while the Jews, not as a people but as a crowd, accept his guilt. Jesus stands before Pilate innocent by Roman law, guilty by Jewish accusation.

For fear of causing another riot—his conduct had caused riots before—Pilate attempts to outsmart the Jews by having Jesus scourged (perhaps working upon their sense of pity) and exposing him to the crowd, "Behold the man!" He isn't troubled about having Jesus whipped with knotted or metal-tipped leather cords—cruelly and unjustly. He has no use for truth. Before Pilate Jesus shows himself to be the real judge of life. His scourging—a compromise—was a normal sentence before death by crucifixion. Jesus is already weakened but doesn't die by this death penalty.

Since no formal charge according to Roman law is brought against Jesus, Pilate simply hands Jesus over to the Roman soldiers for crucifixion. Later Pilate is surprised to hear that Jesus is already dead. He gives permission for his body to be removed from the cross and to be buried.

We are indebted to the Jewish historian Philo for a depiction of the character of Pilate: hot-headed, hateful of the Jews, guilty of illegal killings. Pilate's career comes to a halt when he ruthlessly suppresses Samaritans and is removed from office.

Several questions regarding Pilate remain unanswered: Did he commit suicide? Was he executed? Was he a Christian at heart?

The conflict and issue that still exists all around is between politics and religion, the cowardice of the Caesars in the face of religious truth.

Reflection-prayer

Pontius Pilate, you remind us of our duty to God *and* country. We should like to be free to practice our religion and prove ourselves to be loyal citizens. As Catholics we want to be among the best citizens of our land.

We believe our full and future citizenship to be in the kingdom of heaven.

We belong to a nation whose political leaders speak of our "super-power." If this is not only a political hyperbole, the moral question still rises for us in debate: What qualifies us to be a "super-power"?

I pray that we as a people acknowledge ours to be a nation under God, and that we really do trust in God and in the keeping of his commandments, especially over and above man-made laws.

I do pray continually that we may be governed by honest, just, trustful, peaceful leaders.

5

The Crowd of Spectators

"Crucify him! Crucify him!" Or, "Away with him! Away with him! Crucify him!" How much different is such a mob shout from ours, "Kill the bum!" Anyhow, it's a far cry from the acclamation and applause that echoes out Jesus' recent triumphal entry into Jerusalem.

How much different from us were the crowds who kept shouting to Jesus, "Hosanna! Blessed is he who comes in the name of the Lord! Blessed is the king of Israel!" How does one characterize a crowd? By its shouts? Outcries?

The *Catechism of the Catholic Church* has this description: "The People of God is marked by characteristics that clearly distinguish it from all other religious, ethnic, political or cultural groups in history . . ." (#782).

How many Hebrews in the two crowds earlier rallied around Jesus in their synagogues or in the great outdoors when they heard him preaching to and teaching them? Whenever gathered in groups, must they answer for how they act as a single personality?

Were they the same who in great numbers sought him out, followed and brushed against him when he had them sit in groups and fed them?

It is worth our while to "join" the crowds if only to keep tabs on their reaction as they gather around him, and to feel out the society of the time? Jesus puts the same question to us as he does to the crowds: "Are we with him or against him? Do we gather with him or scatter?"

Jesus faces numerous crowds in the course of his lifetime. Once he establishes his reputation as a preacher and teacher, they flock to him because his words ring true. For the moment at least they believe in him and his message. For them to continue to believe in him is to become the new Israel, the Church. He teaches them the principles of a covenantal relationship, of social justice.

The occasion for the crowds to come to the city of Jerusalem is, first of all, to celebrate the Passover. Some of their number are surprised to hear and see that Jesus is arraigned for trial as a seditionist. The fear spreads that a riot may break out in his behalf. Other Jews, however, hateful of him, are willing to shoulder the blame for his arrest.

In that crowd, as in every crowd, there are simple-intentioned spectators who look on out of curiosity, sightseers. Others are the religious rulers who mock Jesus and bring the charge against him, that of blasphemy which by Hebrew law requires the death penalty, capital punishment, by stoning. Others are Roman soldiers who, knowing no better, join in the mockery while having to keep the crowd under control.

The crowd sees Jesus seated by Pilate mockingly as king and judge. We who live in a democratic society can hardly appreciate what the unity of kingship under a king meant to the people of Israel. One of the functions of a king such as Solomon in Israelitic history was to be a judge. The crowd shouts at Pilate that they will report him to emperor Tiberius unless he convicts Jesus as a pretender to kingship. They have no king but Caesar. This charge upon conviction by a Roman magistrate condemns Jesus to crucifixion, but not according to their own Jewish law.

At first the crowd is more concerned about keeping the Passover unblemished than about crucifying an innocent victim.

But their rabble-rousing leaders see in Jesus an enemy to their religion and are bound to be rid of him, to hasten his death by crucifixion and keeping the Passover "clean." Jesus is doomed as an outcast of his own people, an "individual" who has lost his security among his own people.

What moral and ethical responsibility do crowds have, especially if they are manipulated? How are we to compare their liability to our public protests, rallies, demonstrations, riots, and strikes?

Is there anything "racial" in their hostility to Jesus? Is there something of a spirit of anti-Semitism in the gospel account of the trial and sentence of Jesus? Is the label later applied to the remaining crowd—"Christ-killers"—justifiable?

The crowd—whatever its composition—which stands in judgment of Jesus, represents all who hate and reject Jesus, eventually crucified and risen, namely the evil society of men and women. They must face Jesus as judge, and the judgment upon them is their own refusal of the Light of the world and the saving Word of truth.

Their problem then is one of unbelief. They are wedged into an intermediate state, moral and spiritual, a judgment between Jesus assumed to be the Messiah prophesied and expected from of old, and declared to be the Son of the Most High.

Does the same crowd of witnesses at the trial and judgment of Christ also see him mocked and crucified? And what are their reactions to this spectacle? Does it move their hearts? Evidently at first the crowd isn't shocked at the sight of Jesus torn and bloody. Jeering at him and revolting against him they become his persecutors.

In the final scene his onlookers have to turn away sorrowful, beating their breasts, for guilt is an infectious disease.

As passion and cross are the lot of the Son of God, so persecution is the lot of his followers. Persecution purifies the sinners and tests the just in the assembly of his followers. Sorrow for sin and its expression are characteristic of the true followers of Christ.

Reflection-prayer

We might ask ourselves whether we ever fall back into a crowd-like state of mind when we find fault with, protest, and turn against the Church, the body of Christ. We may all start life with faith, then stop short of a fulfillment of that faith, showing a mob-like hardness of heart or blank-faced personal indifference.

Belonging to the Church, the People of God, as I do, I can feel with the "crowd" of his believers. On a Good Friday or for any act of worship I profess my faith. I should not stand by non-committal.

On the other hand, as a sinner I am numbered in the crowd which has to beat its breast. Before the innocent Christ I must confess my personal sinfulness and collective guilt for the act of crucifixion. I must acknowledge my social responsibility, and not hide unrepentant in a crowd, individualistically.

Alongside Christ crucified I am thankful to be in the midst of the humanity suffered for and forgiven by Christ.

6

Barabbas

The name "Barabbas" is notorious in New Testament history. The name even *sounds* ominous; it might be a villain's name in a stage drama. As it stands, the name is translatable from the Hebrew into "son of the father," harmless of itself. In some ancient manuscripts of his Gospel, St. Matthew refers to him as "Jesus Barabbas," but out of reverence for the name "Jesus" the evangelist Mark drops the name. It's out of character to translate "Barabbas" into "Jesus, son of the father."

Barabbas first appears in the biblical story during the trial of Jesus before Pontius Pilate. He is brought forward by religious authorities in exchange for Jesus, because of their jealousy and the influence Jesus has over the Jewish people. Barabbas is a clever choice by the religious leaders who see an opportunity to be rid of Jesus. They sway the crowd of blind, hateful Jews to prefer Barabbas to Jesus. The crowd acts irresponsibly, for they have no substitute for Jesus in mind. They only want paschal amnesty for a political prisoner. They know the custom was for the "procurator" to release a prisoner on the occasion of a festival. So the responsibility, the evangelist Mark suggests, rests "fairly and squarely" on the shoulders of the chief priests who persuade the crowd to favor Barabbas.

Previously, did Barabbas take part in the movement against Pontius Pilate for transferring funds from the Temple (at Jerusalem) to build an aqueduct to improve the Jerusalem water supply? Possibly. But there is much more reputed about Barabbas than the gospel reports. He may have been something of a national hero for rising up against Roman rule, a liberation fighter. Nowadays we might term him a guerrilla warrior like Ernesto "Che" Guevara, a revolutionist who fought for the Cuban leader Fidel Castro and was mysteriously killed in South America.

The fact is that Barabbas was jailed with rebels who had committed murder during the uprising. There may have been not only political issues at stake here but economic as well, for Barabbas is also accused of robbery (as distinct from thievery!). At any rate, he was a jailbird whom the gospel-writer Matthew calls "a notorious prisoner."

There's a broader background we must see here, namely, the earlier history of the Roman Empire (27 B.C.–A.D. 284), when Israel's land and people were subject to ancient Rome. A tussle issues between Roman civil authority and Jewish religious authority. The Prefect Pontius Pilate ("procurator" was a later title) considers Jesus innocent—he must have been judging by Roman law—and sees how the Jewish leaders are jealous of him. Jesus himself taught that under Roman law citizens should render to Caesar the things that are Caesar's. Jesus himself was a divine lawgiver, and still he orders his purse-keeper to pay the Roman tax.

Apparently in Jesus' time there was need for a more humane political economy. Could there have been, early in the history of Roman imperialism, some of the defects or drawbacks of colonialism? How indicative is it that Barabbas is caught in Pilate's "cold war" with the chief priests?

When the crowd is instigated by the priests to ask for Barabbas in exchange for Jesus, Pilate, to satisfy the crowd and prevent a riot, releases Barabbas to the crowd. Barabbas disappears and is never heard from again.

Here we see that terrible, unjust substitution of the innocent for the guilty, the sinless Savior for the sinful criminal, sponsored by religious authority.

The implications of this injustice are deeper than we may think back into history, for they have to do with Church-state relationships in our own time. The Barabbas incident should give us second thoughts about how to interpret that relationship. The preference is given to Barabbas, and he may well personify the effect of crime and violence in our contemporary society. They work harm upon the innocent and havoc upon society at large. To release the guilty without due punishment or grant pardon is no solution.

And the daily news reports of crime and violence in lurid detail are enough to sicken and sadden any society.

We have, happily, a "book" full of good news to counteract the bad.

Reflection-prayer

Barabbas, your brief but personal history is a sorry-looking blot upon the pages of the Bible.

The trade-off between yourself and Jesus is unjust. Sometimes your rebellious spirit brings harm to innocent citizens.

Your personification of some of the criminals in our society who make the headlines of our daily newspapers causes us fear and distrust and dramatizes evil.

I pray that men and women like you will have a change of heart rather than become repeated offenders, unrepentant.

I ask the Lord's and my neighbors' forgiveness for any injustices I myself have committed. I intend to uphold every kind of justice.

7

Roman Soldiers

T he crucifixion of Jesus took place during the Roman oc-
cupation and domination of Palestine, which we have
noted. It was a criminal punishment adapted from an
Oriental practice but prohibited for Roman citizens by Roman
law, normal only for slaves, bandits, and rebels. Jesus was crucified
by Roman soldiers outside the city walls of Jerusalem by members of a military cohort consisting of six hundred soldiers when
at full force.

Such is the historical fact. His wasn't the first crucifixion
of its kind. Pretenders to the messiahship had been crucified
before him.

Were any of these soldiers present when John the Baptist
confronted them about their duties? They were ordered not to
bully anyone, to accuse no one falsely, and to be content with
their pay. The threefold advice indicated the temptations they
were characteristically to face in their mode of life.

The first step of the soldiers is to bring Jesus into the
courtyard and begin to mock him for his so-called kingship
(perhaps they had first heard of it from King Herod). They
scorn him when he sits down with scepter and reed as on a
throne, and spit on him.

The soldiers begin their manhandling of him after Pilate has him scourged. Scourging is a routine before crucifixion. They scourge him almost to death. They then pick long thorns (firewood) stored in the courtyard and arrange them into a wreath-like crown such as is worn by Greek kings, like a royal diadem depicted on coins, or more likely like a laurel wreath in recognition of the king's military power. It is similar to the crown on the Statue of Liberty.

They don Jesus with a purple cloak, the color of royalty and Roman aristocracy, and they themselves are cloaked in scarlet.

Accusing him falsely (though they may not know better), they make cruel sport of him, "Hail, King of the Jews," out of contempt for his alleged kingship and his people, Jews in general. This scene before us has mysterious but meaningful interpretation. At the same time that Jesus is acclaimed scornfully as king, he fulfills his royal duty of dying for the salvation of his people. Here the passion narrative touches upon the theme of his *divine* kingship.

The Roman military loads Jesus with the crossbeam and then, seeing the weight too much for him to bear, has the right of forcing someone to carry the cross with him.

After nailing Jesus to the cross, and during the crucifixion, the soldiers offer him a share of the drink they carry with them: a cheap, thirst-quenching, sour wine. They lift up to his lips on a spear-point a sponge-filled "quench" to his dying thirst, one of the worst pains of the crucifixion. The apostle John interprets this kind gesture as fulfillment of Ps 69:22: "Rather they put gall in my food and in my thirst they gave me vinegar to drink." It is to finish his life.

To verify Jesus' death, one soldier thrusts his spear into the right side of Jesus, letting blood and water flow out of the wound. Unbeknown to him it is a symbolic act. Jesus continues ever afterward to let his grace flow like water and blood from the sacraments of baptism and Eucharist.

Earlier, in the courtyard, the squad of soldiers had the privilege of dividing Jesus' garments for themselves, which leaves him entirely nude. Then he is re-dressed in an under-garment and seamless tunic. At the foot of the cross the centurion and four soldiers gamble for, i.e., divide by lot, the seamless tunic and garment—"the spoils of war." (Are they discontent with their pay?) Once again, in the gambling for clothes, there is a fulfillment of Scripture: Ps 22:19: ". . . they divide my garments among them, and for my vesture they cast lots." Possibly too the seamless robe is for us symbolic of the unity to be maintained in the Church.

As a result of their witnessing his brave death, the centurion and soldiers profess their belief that Jesus is the Son of God. They exemplify how spiritual combat can win over physical constraint. Jesus, in turn, by his dying on the cross overthrows the prince of evil in the world. His cross proves to be a singlehanded victory for peace far more powerful than any war, a peace pagan Rome cannot bring to its empire.

As an aftermath soldiers are stationed to guard the tomb of Jesus for fear that his body will be stolen and then announced to have risen from the dead. Contrary to their soldierly duty, they are said to have fallen asleep on the job! And the story is told that they experienced an empty tomb and then were bribed to keep their mouths shut about it!

On occasion Jesus showed respect for soldiery but still maintains in his Church the essentially religious character of the life-struggle. Soldiers for Christ are to use Christian virtues for weapons in earthly warfare. Christ himself is the leader of a militant Church, trying always to establish peace with God and among humans: a triumph of his own.

Reflection-prayer

To serve in the military is a patriotic duty. In our past hardly an American family has not experienced it. We still stand in attention and admiration before military parades on national holidays.

The moral question we must bear in mind is whether all acts of war and strikes are justifiable, whether they make for peace, and whether men and women do not die unnecessarily.

Truly a defensive war can be morally justifiable. Nuclear and chemical power, however, is so great and widespread today as to threaten and possibly wipe out a nation or even sweep the earth, leaving no distinction between combatants and non-combatants.

We pray and work for peace before the enormous threat of warfare.

Let us keep conscientiously in mind the dreadful history of war during the last century of the second millennium.

We do belong to a militant Church where spiritual combat against evil is the order of the day, and we do have a lifelong enlistment in God's service.

8

Simon of Cyrene

S imon's biblical portrait, a mere "snapshot," is so brief we
can scarcely delineate it. He is perhaps the least known
of the characters here, a somewhat enigmatic figure and
yet of spiritual importance to us. He enters into the life of Jesus
at its end, and then he is never heard of again. A man of truly
singular appearance, in a humble encounter.

He hailed originally from Cyrene, the capital of Libya in
North Africa. A Jewish colony existed there, dating back to the
fourth century B.C. At the time of the crucifixion, he may have
been a resident of Jerusalem, with his two sons Alexander and
Rufus, or a diaspora Jew on a visit to the holy city for the Passover feast. In either case, he is drawn into our story as a total
stranger. The claim is that his two sons must have been members of the Roman Church. He himself, as later legend has it, is
endowed with a bishopric in Bosra, Africa, where he dies as a
martyr.

Later, his countrymen the Cyrenians were divided among
themselves as followers or opponents of the deacon Stephen.

Simon the Cyrenian has the distinction of belonging to the
oldest and largest part of the Gospel, the passion narrative.

The centerpiece of the passion narrative, the way of the cross is up the rocky hill of Golgotha outside the city gate and alongside an old road where one can meet passers-by. How far actually does Jesus have to carry the cross? The estimate of the distance is not more than a quarter of a mile. What Jesus has to carry is the crossbeam, for there are any number of uprights on the hill where there were countless crucifixions later during the Roman persecutions.

Simon is coming home early from work (work in the fields?) to get ready for the Passover when he is "pressed into service" by Roman soldiers. The biblical expression leaves us with a sense of the need of the moment. Roman soldiers have the right to force others into labor. As they lead Jesus on the way out of the city of Jerusalem, they see that Jesus is severely weakened by the scourging and needs help. Others before him have died by scourging. Will Jesus die before crucifixion?

Do Jesus and Simon collaborate in carrying the cross, or does Simon relieve Jesus of its weight, or does Simon shoulder his weight of the cross in step with Jesus? Jesus isn't reluctant to accept Simon's help, intending to carry the cross as the instrument of his triumph over sin, Satan, and death.

For Simon the carrying of the cross is a chivalrous act, though he may not at once understand the full significance of his salvific courage on the cross.

For him it is a kind of crusade, like a knight or soldier at a crucial historical event. He sets an ideal for Christian "crusaders" to follow in later centuries.

From Simon we can derive the impression that each of us is to be a "second Simon," positioned close to Jesus while carrying our own cross. Thanks to Simon, his humble task, we are put in touch with the cross-carrying Jesus.

Reflection-prayer

Simon of Cyrene, though there is very little we know about you personally, your name and deed are still a title to remembrance in our lives. You have gained a greater renown in salvation history by your "casual" contact with Christ than we can ever claim to. You probably were unknown to the Roman soldiers who drew you out of a crowd. We are, by comparison, insignificant followers of Jesus Christ and members of his Church.

Insignificance, however, is or can be a sign and witness of humility.

Humility is that mysterious virtue which has little or nothing to show for itself, excepting the truth about ourselves.

I should like to imitate you, Simon, in your humble service to the Lord.

Jesus, the passion narrative reports nothing of your reaction to Simon's lending you a helping hand. Is this too meant to be a humbling experience?

May we share in the cross as humbly as Simon did and as humbly as you, Jesus, accepted his help.

9

Women of
Jerusalem

T he women of Jerusalem, and womanhood throughout
Hebrew history, were not given their due. To the modern reader who knows of the emancipation of woman-
kind, this initial statement may seem odd, if not wrong or
biased.

In the history overlapping the Old and New Testaments
women are considered to be lowly, weak, and powerless. Some
actually do show themselves to be valiant and faithful: Sarah,
Rebecca, Rachel, Miriam, Deborah, Hannah, Ruth, Judith,
Esther, and the women we are introduced to in the life-story of
Jesus.

Now who are the women of Jerusalem? They are not cate-
gorized as the group that ordinarily attends to the needs of
condemned criminals and prepares spiced wine. Rather they
are the women who accompany Jesus on his journeys into public ministry. Jesus pays special attention to them—see them in
the Gospel of Luke—because they are still held in such low es-
teem in his own time. Because he knows sufferings are the lot
for them and their children, Jesus speaks words of comfort to
them and their families. At this juncture of salvation history

they are in no mood to call upon the mountains and hills to fall upon them.

They are the women who form a partnership with him, a small contingent friendly and compassionate to him. They pass no sentence of condemnation on him as do other characters of the crucifixion or as worldlings do by their sinfulness. They offer sympathetic help to Jesus while Romans legislate his crucifixion. It is their contact and company with Christ, their sensitivity for the outcast, poor, and downtrodden that reveals their true position in the home, church, synagogue, and society then and now. The sight of their sympathy must stir his heart.

The cross as a stumbling block—scandal—doesn't prevent the faithful laywomen from ministering to Jesus, nor their companionship from relieving his lonely death. We should like to learn from them more specifics about their participation in the life and mission of Jesus.

Who are the women of Jerusalem who meet Jesus along his way to Calvary and mourn for him? Mary his mother, Mary Magdalene, Joanna, and Susanna are among them and remain with him to the end of the crucifixion. Do the women already sense that the cross, cruel and disgraceful, is the way to glory?

"Many" women too view silently and prayerfully the crucifixion from afar: Mary his mother, Mary Magdalene, Salome, Mary the mother of James, Joses and her mother, the mother of the Zebedees. Because they have attached themselves to and ministered to Jesus and his apostles, they approach nearer to the cross as the crowd of spectators thins out. They are now gathered at the foot of the cross. During the mystery of the cross what offices of Christ are they to exercise with their gifts and tasks?

Jesus' cross isn't a lost cause for the Jerusalem women. Unlike the apostles they do not disperse and go their individual ways. They are mindful and respectful of the human body even in its death. Their faith immediately leads them from cross to tomb. Soon they are to come to honor the dead and anoint his body with aromatic oils and salves. They give no thought to a closed tomb.

Do they witness or believe in an angel rolling aside the stone blocking its entrance?

The holy and faithful women are enlightened to realize the meaning of the empty tomb. They appear calm and communicative, ready to participate in the life and mission of the Church. At this point of time they are *leading* characters. They are the first to receive the Easter message and announce it to the other disciples.

In due time in his Church Jesus grants women a new dignity and role. Their femininity represents the Church fittingly as it awaits in prayer the Pentecost.

Jesus as the Messiah points to the Old Testament in which God's covenantal relationship with his people is portrayed as a marriage. In the New Testament Jesus accepts the Church as his bride. The women are the "bridesmaids" in the sacrament of his Church. So long as the Bridegroom is in his Church, there is no cause to mourn. The triumph of the cross the Jerusalem women are witness to introduces the new creation and affords eschatological joy.

Reflection–prayer

Handmaids of the Lord, you have been an inspiration to us throughout the priestly, prophetic, and kingly life and work of Christ during his lifetime and now in his Church. I believe our respect, appreciation, and cooperation has its beginning in the home, the domestic church, with our mothers and sisters.

It is obvious that in large measure parochial life, worship, and ministry revolve around the core of women who offer their time, talent, and treasure to it. Their support, spiritual and apostolic, spreads the mission of the Church into the secular society. They embody the Church in her role of bride of Christ.

As Pope John Paul II has invited them, they have yet ever more to establish their dignity and integrity in "re-evangelizing" and "humanizing" social life.

10

The Mother of the Zebedees

Why single out this woman from the other women of Jerusalem. Is there something special about her? I believe there is.

We might overlook her standing not at the foot of the cross but at least within Jesus' earshot or eyeshot of it, with the women who used to attend to Jesus' needs. We do find her first name to be Salome (Mark 15:40; 16:1), we do know that she is the mother of the sons of Zebedee, James and John, possibly cousins of Jesus (if Salome is Mary's sister).

Her sons are the two called by Jesus into his discipleship. Immediately they drop their fishing nets and leave their father. The father is left to shift for himself (at Bethsaida?), and we hear nothing more about him. Fathers and mothers have to step aside to allow their sons to pursue their own vocations. They must have felt the urgency of Jesus' call. They turn out to be two of his very close friends who are to be with Jesus at the most intimate occasions of his life, as on the mount of his transfiguration and in the Garden of Gethsemane.

There are in the Gospels two accounts of the request for the two brothers to have select places in the kingdom of heaven, at the right and left of Jesus. The one account (Mark 10:35ff.) has the two brothers themselves petitioning Jesus and being overheard by the other disciples who resent their pushiness.

The other account (Matt 20:22ff.) is of their mother interceding for them with the same request: privileged places at his side, once he enters into his glory. In either request there is no questioning the glorious future Jesus is to have. Jesus, however, doesn't pull rank; the reward is simply not his to give, it is his Father's.

In both gospel accounts Jesus lets it be known and makes it very clear that to be a follower of his is to take with him the way of the cross. Sacrifice must be the lot of people who strive for greatness. To be truly great is to offer service to others. Jesus says to himself that he came not to be served but to serve.

There can be no doubt that the mother too learned this lesson from the lips of Jesus, although the Markan Gospel leaves the mother out of the picture. Did James and John put their mother up to this request? We do not know, but it is typical of a loving mother to want and seek the best for her sons. Is she seeking the "hundredfold" Jesus promises to those who leave father and mother to follow him? At any rate, we have the powerful and unselfish example of her intercession.

We meet her once more in the Gospel of Matthew (27:56) at the scene of the crucifixion, along with other women. Salome doesn't stand as close to Jesus as her son John (her other son James is absent). But is she close enough to hear or is she informed that Jesus puts his own mother into the home and care of John: "Woman, there is your son," and turning to John, "There is your mother" (John 19:25f.)? Afterward Salome still keeps close to Jesus the crucified, and upon his burial is ready with other women to anoint his body with perfumed oils they had purchased.

When we compare the relationship of the Zebedee family to the threesome at Bethany, Martha, Mary, and Lazarus, we see that it is quite different. It has the feature of a *full* family relationship to him. It is true, other mothers and fathers meet up with Jesus in his life and ministry, but there is something unique about this relationship. It is *family*-oriented. Jesus deals with others on their own terms, besides his own. He isn't persuaded to grant her singular favors because of her service to him.

As a mother, Salome is the giver of life both in the family and in the history of salvation. She is to be respected as much as the father of her sons.

How much of their *filial* piety is due to her motherhood? There certainly is evidence in the Gospel of Jesus that she stood by her sons in the establishment of a community of believers. During their ministry to the early Church and their gathering with Jesus of a community of women disciples, they express the fruitfulness of the "mother" Church, characteristic of their own mother. And we are left to speculate how much after the resurrection of Jesus she was a comfort to his mother. Was she present with Mary and other women in the upstairs room at Jerusalem and devoting herself to prayer? Truly theirs was a community of women disciples devoted to Jesus and with the men forming a family of disciples.

In the Gospel of John women disciples are given prominence and seemingly equated with the twelve apostles. Whenever John speaks of "we," he is including the entire community. Discipleship is what John has most in mind, both of women and men. According to his own thought and plan for his community, the ideal of discipleship is to include women.

Reflection–prayer

Jesus, I pray that I may be as ready always to follow you as were the sons, James and John.

I thank you for the motherhood of Mary in the Church, and for my own mother, her example and intercession.

May I always be respectful of the women disciples in the modern-day community of believers.

I should like to give as much priestly service as possible to the women organizations in the Church.

Keep me mindful of the family—the domestic church—in the structure and life of the parish.

11

The Two Thieves

The two thieves find themselves at the edge of life, beside a "man" they may never have met before but, seemingly, not a complete stranger. At this crucial moment of their lives they are literally "thick as thieves," yet not committing crimes for the sake of an easy life, entertainment or gain. Apparently, they have no family members, relatives, or friends to stand by them—a lonely death is theirs. It would be instructional to know about their upbringing, their strengths and weaknesses derived from their parents and/or teachers.

They were led along with Christ, bearing their own crossbeams, and then crucified, the one on his right, the other on his left. (The one is sometimes frescoed with a devil hovering over him, the other with an angel.) They finally disagree among themselves.

Curiously, the great Arizona artist and sculptor Ted De Gratia in one of his paintings appears to have placed both criminals on the *left* of Jesus. Two insurgents against Roman rule—they are noted not only for thievery—taunt Jesus the proclaimed king of the Jews to come down from the cross and rescue them.

The second charge against them, thievery, still keeps them nailed to the cross. The seventh commandment of God, "You shall not steal," holds by natural law for everybody, believers or not, and the Roman law upholds its truth, has the right to regulate and enforce it, and punish offenders against it. Cattle stealing is seen to be the worst offense. Restitution is to be made for stolen or damaged goods and property. The thief unable to pay back may be sold into slavery, so strict the restitution. Or for a very serious crime he may be given the death penalty.

One of the criminals speaks up and blasphemes Jesus for not doing his messianic duty of saving himself and the two of them. The other, Dismas by his traditional name, has a change of heart and rebukes him for his lack of fear of God. The interchange between the two is briefly characteristic of the struggle between good and evil. Though under the same sentence as Jesus, they deserve punishment; he's innocent. Then the repentant thief asks Jesus to remember him upon entering his reign. Jesus assures him of paradise that very day (before sunset).

The "good" thief has this "last-minute" conversion to Christ, perhaps when he recalls hearing about Jesus or knowing his reputation, then gradually turning to him in his heart. His words to Jesus speak the language of hope, which he keeps repeating. He acknowledges Jesus' innocence and recognizes him as a true Messiah. What he asks for is to be included in kingly power when Jesus returns. Jesus will then inaugurate the messianic age, extending to the resurrection of the dead. He promises the good thief a share in his royalty.

In this crucifixion-event, with Jesus situated between two thieves, good and bad, and in their words as reported in the Scripture, a kind of judgment is taking place. Whether we sense it or not, it relates to us. A saving factor for us lies in Jesus' intervention for us upon the cross.

The good thief feels a bond with the dying Christ. He wants to be dying in Christ. His union with the Savior reminds us Christians that we too are "crucified" with Christ. As the good thief experiences the mercy of Christ, so do we.

Christ's promise to the good thief—a place in his kingdom—points to the parable of the poor man Lazarus and to the parousia, Christ's second coming at the end of the world. Time is running out for the three crucified, and the parousia is fast approaching for them. For Christ and the good thief the cross is an early triumphal phase of the parousia, and a sign relating them to us.

The soldiers standing by have yet to administer the coup de grace to the two thieves by breaking their legs, for they are still alive to hear Jesus' last words. Nothing is reported about the garments they leave behind, which by right belong to the executioners (in this curious twist of justice).

We must listen to Jesus' last words about his second coming in the context of an earlier statement of his, that he will come at the parousia like a *thief* in the night—suddenly and unexpectedly.

The good thief isn't caught off guard, dismally. But on his own time he contrasts with the courage and patience we Christians are to hold to in the long run of life in the Church. The kingdom of God is to come within us: "a kingdom of truth and life, a kingdom of holiness and grace, a kingdom of justice, love, and peace."

The paradise which once was man's homeland is now elevated to be the good thief's home, an anticipated and singular triumph of the cross.

By some quirk of history, the good thief Dismas is said to have left a hermitage in Montserrat, Spain, inviting us to pray.

Reflection-prayer

Thank goodness, no thievery of spiritual goods is possible, only a sharing of them and a final happy destiny and inheritance for everyone.

The threat of crime and violence in our cities is no stranger to us. We all are to seek justice of every kind in our society.

The better we keep the just laws of our land, the closer we attain to the kingdom of God.

Honesty, truth, justice serve Christ and build up his kingdom far more efficiently than the man-made laws and courts of our nation.

We need to defend justice in imitation of Jesus' defense of the good thief, and Dismas' own plea for justice.

Last of all, we need to pray in the spirit of Dismas for the grace of a happy death.

12

Mary Magdalene

Mary Magdalene may have been misunderstood in the history of the Church to be someone she was not. Her reputation was that of a great sinner because she was ticketed to be the one out of whom Jesus drove seven devils. But that expression only indicated her very serious illness of which she was cured.

At any rate, the Church honors her as an example of a great penitent. She does let the world know that many are called to follow Christ but few are chosen, as she was, and that men and women must work out their salvation with fear of being lost to the cause of Christ.

Mary is a resident of the town of Magdala (modern Mejdel) in Galilee, situated on the western coast of the sea of Galilee. Galilee is the area where Jesus does most of his preaching and teaching.

She's among the women the evangelist Luke introduces by name. Jesus shares his ministry with her in order to spread the good news of the kingdom of God. Along with the other women Magdalene contributes to it out of her means. Little else is known about her until . . . .

Mary is "entrusted" with the witness to the last events in the human and earthly life of Jesus: that is how John in his Gospel overlaps the crucifixion of Jesus with his resurrection, ascension, and glorification.

She's named too among the faithful women who stand at the foot of the cross, bearing witness to the crucified Christ, and later to his burial and resurrection. Her women companions think of the spices they are to buy for the anointing of Jesus' body.

Early on a Sunday morning while it was still dark, Mary goes directly to Nicodemus' tomb and notices that the stone is rolled away from the entrance, but she is unable to look into it. She is in tears that "they" have removed him from the tomb. She stoops and peers inside and discovers two dazzling angels there, one at the foot and the other at the head of the place where Jesus was lain. Love-inspired for him and unconcerned about herself, she inquires about the whereabouts of his body. She isn't sure but that "they" have absconded with his body.

When he first appears to her, she doesn't recognize the risen Christ, assuming him to be the garden's owner or overseer. He can inform her about the disturbance of the tomb and why it should be empty. A twelfth-century painting on wood has Jesus standing as a gardener with shovel in hand.

The risen Christ has only to address Mary by name for her to be the first to recognize him. Mary throws herself at Jesus' feet and wraps her arms around his knees to demonstrate her belief and love. Jesus, though, not wanting Mary to cling to him, makes it known to her that he has yet to finish his glorification. She then dashes off by herself to contact other disciples, Peter and John. She is "an apostle to the apostles."

The sequence of events here and now is hard to determine, but one thing is sure: Jesus, known well by Mary in his crucifixion, in his resurrection is no magical illusion to her.

Mary, the joyful witness to the risen Christ, isn't believed at first, yet we are indebted to her for the initial belief and spread of belief in his resurrection.

Notably, Jesus risen doesn't show himself to throngs of people—to four or five thousand, nor to those responsible for his execution, only to select witnesses, his close, intimate followers, to a few faithful Israelites.

Because Mary Magdalene thinks only of Jesus in this post-resurrection situation, St. Teresa of Avila calls Mary an "audacious" witness. After his ascension, according to tradition, she bears witness to him in France. Her solitary testimony ought to embolden his followers everywhere.

Reflection-prayer

Mary Magdalene, it's encouraging that your tears of sorrow turn into a witness of joy for your Savior.

Your ready witness follows closely upon the triumphal course of the cross.

It seems, however, that in the history of salvation devotion to you rose but slowly.

It should teach us that we too must be "audacious" in our pursuit of Christ, his grace, and virtue.

For your saintliness rests well upon the witness of angels and the appearance of the risen "Rabboni."

With the help of your prayers we join you in bearing the good news of salvation to others who have yet to believe in the resurrection of Jesus.

We pray with you for all who have dedicated themselves to singlehood in the service of the Lord and his Church.

13

John, Son of Zebedee

There are three "clues" in his Gospel to gaining an understanding of the eminent character of John, son of Zebedee, born at Bethsaida. The first and perhaps the most memorable is his use of the word "hour." The second is the "signs" he refers to, which have a touch of mystery about them. And the third is the repeated phrase "lifted up" in chapters 3, 8, and 12. We will explore their meanings more carefully, for they indicate that his writings are more impressionistic than biographical.

The "hour" associated John with his master Jesus, although Jesus speaks of it earlier when at the wedding feast of Cana he "postpones" it for his mother. We should recall that Jesus took some of his apostles with him on that occasion. Did John overhear the remark to Mary? John keeps it in mind, being the only apostle to witness Jesus bearing the cross.

Jesus' "hour" spans the events of his crucifixion, death, resurrection, and glorification. It marks one phase of his glorification, when he triumphs over sin, death, and Satan—sin, the pervasive cause of his death. Jesus cries out his accomplishment on the cross: "the finishing touch" to his "signs": his works and miracles. His Father gives success to the work of his hands. His "hour" extends itself through the life of his Church, for the one depends in true faith upon the other.

The "signs" John points to are in his sight symbolic: they have a broader meaning in his ministry than in the miracles of Jesus. They endow us as they did John himself with the spiritual goods of grace and virtue. They are Jesus' media of communication with John and with us. They convey truth and life.

For John the "lifting up" of Jesus on the cross links him up with his further movements of resurrection, ascension, and glorification. In his spiritual sense of it he compenetrates, i.e., links and fuses together the last events in the life of Jesus without regard to time and place. They are not so much successive historical events as a growing reality, an ascending movement of the Son to the Father, sweeping us up into his victory. The cross of Christ is a sign of victory over sin, death, and Satan. John beholds in his master an exaltation counterpoised to a humiliation, as contrary as that may seem to us. The fact is noteworthy that John places the key phrase "lift up" on Jesus' lips ("I will draw all men to myself"), foretelling Jesus' own experience of suffering defeat at human hands while experiencing joy in his victory by divine power, a mystical paradox.

How is it that the three—"hour, signs, lifting up"—are so characteristic of this son of Zebedee, and hardly mentionable in the life of other apostles, including John's own brother James? We shall see.

A fisherman by trade, John spends his early years in the company of his father and brother. He and his brother James are nicknamed "Sons of Thunder," seemingly because of their fiery character. On one occasion they get all fired up against the Samaritans. Does this temperament instill in John a sense of urgency for that "hour" which is still to come?

He and his brother James had been disciples of John the Baptist before joining Jesus in his ministry. That intimacy also unties them from their families. John remains a witness to Jesus from the day of the forerunner John's baptism of Jesus in the river Jordan till his ascension. The three of them—Peter, James, and John—are to be with Jesus at the most crucial moments of his life: the Last Supper, in the Garden of Gethsemane, and his trial.

John, moreover, is identified as "the beloved disciple" of Jesus. He assumes a place to the right of Jesus at the table of the Last Supper, so close to Jesus as to be privy to Jesus' naming his betrayer. This closeness to Jesus entitles him to be the "author" of the Johannine tradition, which we have already acknowledged to be full of spiritual insight, creating a spiritual theology. It is this tradition so characteristic of the beloved disciple we Christians are heir to, rich as it is for spiritual life.

John would have us view the Last Supper—the Eucharist—as a wedding feast celebrating Jesus as the Bridegroom of the Church. The feast is the Church's sign or sacrament reminiscent of the Jewish Passover but "passing over" into Christian life.

Neither John nor the other apostles realize fully the meaning of the cup of suffering Jesus alludes to. They are first-hand witnesses to the night trial before the Jewish leader Annas, a sort of high-priestly patriarch. John himself remains unnamed but known to the High Priest in his courtyard.

Later John takes his stance at the foot of the cross. He senses the power of Christ overcoming the evil spirit once and for all. The great moment of salvation history arrives, a climax to the "hour" of Christ rising from the cross into glory, an apogee which glorifies us.

Because it is Jesus' own role in the Church, which is to make a supreme sacrifice of himself, John purposes to be like a slave-leader in the Church, to suffer the sight of the Crucified and the burdensome will of others, even though martyrdom is not his lot. He thinks of himself too as a prophet, servant of the Lord, brother and companion in tribulation. He wants us to believe that in church-life we are indeed gifted with the very life of Christ, whatever it entails. We are to think *with* him, for he himself thinks independently of other authors in the New

Testament. The longer we live in the Church, the more fully we come to terms with his Gospel.

He is one of the founders of and decision-makers in the early Church, one of the select three who witness more salvific events than others do. He and the other apostles are to "fill in" till Jesus' return at the end of time. His memory helps him to record the missionary works of the last third of the first century.

John may have traveled outside Palestine; he may have once lived in Asia Minor on the island of Patmos, banished there by Roman authorities.

How prolific a writer he was is a matter in much dispute. His authorship of the Fourth Gospel, the three letters under his name, and the book of Revelation still keeps biblical students divided in opinion. The Johannine writings do bear the stamp of his authority.

His writings win him the title of "theologian." They truly are spiritual writings, lending themselves to the contemplation of Christ, "the Lamb" and "the Word of God." The words and deeds of Jesus are to be understood now with the light of the Holy Spirit and in the tradition of the Church, seen as the sacrament of Christ.

Reflection-prayer

I am grateful to you, John, for the spiritual theology you have left us to contemplate with.

Since we are to follow Christ, our master, you have engaged us in living out the "hour" of Christ crucified.

The "signs" in our Christian life are the cause for us to believe in Christ. His sacraments reveal how he lives in us, in his Church.

You continue to teach us that Christ "lifts" us up with himself as we accompany him along the glorious way of the cross.

Most of all, it is your spiritual message that we long for in our hearts.

14

Mary, Mother of Jesus

"Or take the lilies; they do not spin, they do not weave, but I tell you, Solomon in all his splendor was not arrayed like any one of these" (Luke 12:27).

The so-called Madonna lily is a flower growing in the Holy Land and beautifying the countryside. It catches the eye of Jesus and invites his comment: the Madonna lily outdoes Solomon in his splendor. It is also called the Annunciation lily, which no doubt derives its name from the event in the life of the Virgin Mary, Jesus' mother, the Madonna of Nazareth and Jerusalem, translated into "my Lady," who becomes in the Church "our Lady." Whatever Mary had to spin or weave for the family of Nazareth could not have been arrayed as she was—"full of grace."

The painter Raphael's Sistine Madonna with its halo suggests a sense of mystery hovering over Mary, the mystery of her bringing Jesus from eternity into time, from the divine to the human, to us. We shall explore her mystery in his life and ours.

To contemplate her role in the crucifixion of her son, we do have to go back to two significant sites, first and last, in her life: Cana and Calvary. Otherwise she stays in the background of her Son's ministry. At Cana, where Mary is respectful of the newlyweds and sensitive to their needs, she introduces Jesus into his ministry. Mary is again at his side at the finish of his ministry on Calvary. At Cana Mary calls upon the resourcefulness of her Son, which comes to completion on the cross. Mary's power of intercession with her Son sweeps through his ministry to the last, his "hour," while she is standing by him, without playing a part in his public life as the "first" of his disciples.

As it is for every young lady, the retention of her virginity is a sacrifice for Mary and it remains a gift from God the Father in the motherhood of her Son. Hers too is an act of humble obedience to the will of God in her life. Mary, by her consent to motherhood, joins with Jesus in the divine plan of salvation.

Not only does she conceive Jesus by the power of the Holy Spirit, but the Spirit enables her to come to an ever better understanding of her Son "Emmanuel"—"God is with us." She cannot help but notice the glint of light or suggestion of God's presence in her divine-human Son. The realization dawns upon her that he is more than human. Through growth in faith she comes to realize personally how God has a hand in her life and by the gift of faith is achieving the salvation of the world.

Jesus is first recognized in public, locally, as the carpenter, "the son of Mary," which may have been an insult but could have been handed down to us in a faulty manuscript record. Mary, a Semite, is impressed ever more by the divine power and goodness in the words and works of Jesus as he grows older. She "ponders" them again and again, by the light of the Holy Spirit.

Thus in a spirit of faith Mary cooperates with her Son in his redemptive role. Her faith is characterized, as ours is, by a degree of obscurity when she meets with Simeon and Anna, for she doesn't yet have a beatific vision of her Son. Her own prayerfulness and reflection helps her to accept her role alongside his. Her role is unobtrusive and her character self-effacing. Mary's prayer life gradually develops into silent contemplation the closer she accompanies Jesus to the crucifixion. She keeps pondering the mystery of his life and action.

Jesus is confronted early by the disbelief and disrespect of his countrymen, though not all. Mary witnesses her people's rejection of her Son even in his hometown where the townspeople should know him better. She may not always understand her Son at the spur of the moment (at age twelve his staying behind in the Temple), but she does advance in her pilgrimage of faith from his conception to crib to cross. She follows her Son faithfully as the first of his disciples.

To Israel Jesus' dying on the cross is a scandal. To Mary, however, standing at the side of her crucified Son, it is a co-suffering. Predictably, a sword of sorrow pierces her soul just as a spear is thrust into his side. For the sake of peace the sword should be beaten into a ploughshare, the spear into a pruning hook.

During his dying moments, his "hour," Jesus stays aware of his mother, makes her his first beneficiary, and addresses her once again as "woman" for her to be a symbol of the Church and the mother of Christians (whom the beloved disciple personifies). Also it is in his being "lifted up" that Mary becomes our Queen-mother. Mary is mother of us all because it is through her Son that we are adopted as children of God, given a spiritual kinship. Jesus continues to act in his Church through his mother, in her exercise of a spiritual motherhood.

At last Mary rejoins her Son in the "hour" of his agony for the sins of humankind and the ecstasy of commending his spirit to the Father. To the very last of his life, she proves herself to be the handmaiden of the Lord. She "was associated more intimately than any other person in the mystery of his redemptive suffering" (*Catechism of the Catholic Church*, #618).

Reflection-prayer

Mary, you are our Mother of sorrows and our Lady of joy.

In our crucible of sorrows, we appeal to you and are grateful to you for our joys. Our joys keep us in mind of your part in the wedding feast at Cana, and our sorrows of your stance on Calvary and your share in the crucifixion of your Son.

We should like to ponder repeatedly the mystery of Jesus in your life and your mystery in ours.

We pray to you in the family of the Church that we may be obedient children of yours.

You are both our Madonna lily and Mystical rose in the new Jerusalem, the Church. We pray, Mary, that you will mother us to advance in the virtues of purity and charity.

We honor you as a Queen-mother because you are mother of a king.

15

Christ Crucified

The cross is described in the Bible as "the tree of life." It is one of the many meanings attached to this symbol, suggesting paradoxically that by this means—a fruitful death—the Savior Jesus Christ brings to us the life of grace, a share in his own divine life. It stands in contrast to the tree of forbidden fruit that tempted the first man and woman.

The *Catechism of the Catholic Church* puts this teaching simply: "By his glorious Cross Christ has won salvation for all men" (#1741). Hanging upon the cross Christ bestows upon humankind the gift of himself, a gift of love to atone for human selfishness and sinfulness. From crib to cross Jesus lives the life of the "poor," the last of the various degrees of poverty which characterize his life. He fulfills his own teaching to the *anawim:* "How blest are the poor in spirit; the reign of God is theirs."

His way of the cross is forecast by John the Baptist in the watery baptism of Jesus at the river Jordan, anticipating his bloody baptism on the cross, and begins already when he is rejected by his townspeople, betrayed by a friend, and deserted by his disciples. He is ridiculed by fellow religionists, Roman soldiers heap mockery upon him, and he is taunted by a thief. Time-wise, the outreach of the cross is not only into the past but into the near-and-far future, *our* future. The way itself, traveled afoot, is only about a quarter-mile. It ends up on Golgotha hill, the name translated into the Place of the Skull.

How are we to assess wisely the meaning of the cross in our life, lest we be foolish? The cross-event was, to be sure, and still is, foolish in the eyes of unbelievers. A horrible event, it was because of the Crucified unparalleled in human history. For wise believers it was and remains a salvific event. God the Father recognizes his Son to be a liberator and savior. Jesus in dying on the cross fulfills the will of his heavenly Father. He isn't simply a victim of political and/or religious circumstance.

In the characterization of Christ nailed to the cross, we are to see him carrying out three distinct roles, those of priest, prophet, and king.

It is not as if Christ, priest, has to undergo the sacrifice of his life as a last resort to save humankind. He can walk away from it as he once escaped being pitched over a hill. As a priest he offers himself to his heavenly Father and is "lifted up." As a victim feeling abandonment by his Father, he "empties himself," i.e., in death itself. As an act of priest-victim, Jesus bears his cross over into the word and sacrament of the Mass.

His "preface" to the crucifixion is his high-priestly prayer the evening of the Last Supper. It is the offering of himself on the eve of his sacrifice on the cross and his interceding that others may continue his word and work. The longest of his prayers, it conveys the spirit of the priest-victim he is. In it he prays for himself, that he may complete his work of redemption, for his followers that they may attain to eternal life, and that he may achieve his aim of glorifying his Father. He prays especially for his apostles, friends of his, because it is for them that he is willing to sanctify himself. He is a sacrificial victim for them. His prayer makes contact with all who are to come in his footsteps, for their unity, that they may see in him a Shepherd of the flock. His prayer for unity is to succeed in eternal life.

Prophets of old, such as Isaiah and Jeremiah and John the Baptist, who spoke out for God, had to endure death as a consequence of their message. The theme of sacrifice Jesus as prophet preaches and teaches throughout his ministry, inviting his followers to take up the cross, he concludes on the cross and exemplifies his own prophetic message. In his last words he commends himself to his Father.

In the midst of his suffering, Jesus offers consolations to others. He speaks words of forgiveness to his enemies and sinners, and he *repeats* his words. He turns his cross into a "mercy seat" for all sinners.

Up to this point it is for him a royal way of the cross. The title posted above his head states the popular cause of his execution: "Jesus Christ, King of the Jews." Although the purpose of his kingship on the "throne" of the cross is to reign over evil of every kind, it is misunderstood by both Jews and Romans. The Jews reject him as a messiah-king, while to the Romans before whom he is professed to be king of the Jews, he appears to be a rebel against the Roman imperial government. Christ's reign on the cross must be understood to be a spiritual and moral power at work, ruling over nature, sickness, sin, death, and Satan. What seems to be a stumbling block and curse to others is for us the wisdom and power of God, the almighty ruler.

Of all the events in the life of Christ, the cross is the most revelatory. The cross-event, including the "hour" of his passion, death, resurrection, and ascension, is the majestic moment of his triumph, when the Father glorifies his Son, the firstborn of the dead. It is therefore a transcendent Christ-event, transcendent inasmuch as he still ministers to us in the sacraments of his Church.

The Christian symbol of the cross implies for all "cross-bearers" a renunciation of selfishness, entailing a daily struggle, the condition for the discipleship of Jesus. To be "crucified" with Christ is to "fill out" what is lacking in his sufferings, while there is nothing lacking in their overall redemptive value. To find oneself is to lose oneself *in Christ*.

To join in the experience of the crucified, the most singular of characters, the experience must combine the sorrow of the agony with the joy of the victory, a mixture of humiliation and exaltation. The mystery is so deep and diffusive we are hard put to find expression for it, compelling the Christian to resort to poetic language. The Christian experience of the mystery of the Cross is described as "the martyrdom of pain and delight" (St. Teresa of Avila) and as "delicious burnings" and "inebriating wounds." It doesn't occur only in the life of mystics. Christian souls do keep themselves and are kept in peace despite intense and lasting pain. The crucified Savior endows his faithful followers with this paradox of the Cross.

Reflection-prayer

My dear disciple, I have counted you as a companion on my way of the cross, from my betrayal by a friend to my side spear-pierced by a soldier, and I have gifted you with the faith, hope, and love to follow me without fail.

As a sharer in my priesthood you are to offer yourself to God the Father and glory in the holy cross. As a victim, do pray for the courage to bear the cross. It will prove you to be triumphant at the end of your life.

My last words from the cross resound prophetically to you. I trust you will preach and teach in a true spirit of prophesy, after taking my words to heart.

The royal way of the cross entitles you to a place in my kingship, universal and eternal. Meanwhile do intend to rule and judge your life by the laws of God.

As Lord and Savior, I strengthen your faith and encourage you to learn the mystery of the Cross, its pains and delights.

Epilogue

One of the richest words in the English vocabulary is "character." We have been using and understanding it in one of its many meanings, but it has a much richer meaning in the Roman Catholic Church, which the dictionary includes. Although it doesn't spell them out, good character traits include responsibility, respect, kindness, compassion, honesty, integrity, which make for good character development.

Besides his or her personal character, the human person can have, if anointed by the Holy Spirit in one or all three sacraments of the Church—baptism, confirmation, and holy orders—a new, spiritual, sacramental character. The anointing with holy oil, chrism, leaves the person marked forever, indelibly, irrevocably.

By the anointing with oil he/she belongs to and comes from God and the Holy Spirit. Each person is sealed as it were, configured to Christ in order to live a life of faith, witness, and service. The baptismal character is prefigured by Christ at his baptism in the river Jordan and enacted by the baptism of his death, and then is enriched by the Spirit in the confirmational character, and the confirmational by the priestly. From the one to the other there is a gradual but more distinct configuration to Christ, from becoming a child of God to a Christian adult to a priest according to the order of Melchisedek. The Christian character is gifted with more than natural ability to do good.

We can speak then of a "dual" character, sacramental and moral. The sacramental character strengthens the moral, but neither of the two can do much good without pursuing and practicing moral virtues, even to an outstanding degree. Moral virtues are not simply for the asking; they demand long and toilsome practice, like good habits we acquire through strong, lasting effort—certainly not without self-sacrifice, self-discipline.

The difference between the two, the acquisition of virtue and lack of it, is fairly typical in all who play a part in the passion narrative. Good character makes for a power to do good, over and beyond the image and likeness the Creator has put in his every human creature. Bad character lacks the power to do good. The one is empowered to resist temptation and avoid sin, the other is not. The distinction between the two remains evident in every human person.

Christian morality enables anyone and everyone to participate in the crucifixion as a Peter; a Mary Magdalene; a John, son of Zebedee; a mother of the Zebedees; a Mary, mother of Jesus. Not only in the suffering but in the triumph.

Good character traits are ennobled by the crucified Christ, "Christified" so to speak by his victory upon the cross. Men and women of "cruciform character" have a positive, hopeful outlook upon life. They experience a phoenix-like reward in Christ crucified. They must still live and work with the permanent mystery in his redemptive act, "so that the cross of Christ might [be filled] with its meaning" (cf. 1 Cor 1:17).